WILLIAM RANDOLPH HEARST

Publishing Pioneers

WILLIAM RANDOLPH *H*EARST

NEWSPAPER MAGNATE

by Bonnie Z. Goldsmith

Content Consultant:
Stephen Vaughn, Professor of Journalism, University of
Wisconsin–Madison, School of Journalism and Mass Communications

ABDO
Publishing Company

CREDITS

Published by ABDO Publishing Company, 8000 West 78th Street, Edina, Minnesota 55439. Copyright © 2010 by Abdo Consulting Group, Inc. International copyrights reserved in all countries. No part of this book may be reproduced in any form without written permission from the publisher. The Essential Library™ is a trademark and logo of ABDO Publishing Company.

Printed in the United States.

 PRINTED ON RECYCLED PAPER

Editor: Melissa Johnson
Copy Editor: Rebecca Rowell
Interior Design and Production: Darin Anderson
Cover Design: Darin Anderson

Library of Congress Cataloging-in-Publication Data
Goldsmith, Bonnie Zucker.
  William Randolph Hearst : newspaper magnate / by Bonnie Goldsmith.
       p. cm. — (Publishing pioneers)
  Includes bibliographical references and index.
  ISBN 978-1-60453-763-5
  1. Hearst, William Randolph, 1863-1951—Juvenile literature. 2. Publishers and publishing—United States—Biography—Juvenile literature. 3. Newspaper publishing—United States—History—19th century—Juvenile literature. 4. Newspaper publishing—United States—History—20th century—Juvenile literature. I. Title.
  Z473.H4G65 2009
  070.5'092—dc22
  [B]
                                   2009010000

TABLE OF CONTENTS

William Randolph Hearst, shown in 1910, was a newspaper publisher and politician.

A Stolen Election

*G*etting up early was rarely on the agenda for William Randolph Hearst. The most famous newspaperman in the United States usually returned to his *New York American* newsroom at midnight. He would go home at 4:00 a.m. after seeing the morning edition go to press. He worked as hard as any member of his staff, getting his hands full of ink as he worked through the middle of the night on every detail of his newspaper. But Hearst could not sleep late on the morning of November 7, 1905. At the age of 42, he hoped he was about to be elected mayor of New York City.

A Third Party

Hearst had always been a loyal Democrat, but he was convinced by the early 1900s that both major U.S. political parties were equally corrupt. The Democrats had supported his run for U.S. Congress in 1902. This guaranteed his election and his reelection in 1904. But the Democratic Party had not supported Hearst for the presidential nomination in 1904. The party thought Hearst was too ambitious. So Hearst decided to run on his own.

In 1905, Hearst created a new, or third, political party called the Municipal Ownership League and ran for mayor of New York City. His message was always the same.

Famous Progressive Publisher

Hearst burst on the U.S. publishing scene in 1887. That year, at the age of 24, he took over the *San Francisco Examiner.* He turned the newspaper into a huge success by transforming its appearance and dedicating its pages to progressive causes.

If elected, he would take back from big companies what should belong to the city and its citizens, namely, control of vital services. These included water, transportation, ice, gas, and electricity. No more private contracts would enrich certain individuals and raise prices for New Yorkers. Hearst would govern without corruption. He would return government to the people.

A Surprising Campaign

Hearst's experience using newspapers to champion issues helped him run his campaign for mayor. His four New York papers gave lavish coverage of every event. They reported on the huge, wildly cheering crowds Hearst attracted. Hearst's rousing campaign speeches were printed in his newspapers and won him more and more support.

Hearst's history of supporting progressive causes had made him very

A New Journalism

Hearst practiced a new kind of journalism. His papers were politically independent, appealed to a wide range of people, and were produced using the latest printing technology. They featured big, bold, dramatic headlines and many first-rate illustrations. To attract readers, he filled the pages with new features: crime stories, community achievements, advice columns, scandals, sports, and the wildly popular Sunday comics. Hearst sent his investigative reporters on crusades against corrupt government. Through his publications, he passionately supported labor unions and fought to improve the lives of ordinary working people.

popular among working people. His opponents were alarmed. The Socialist Party reminded people that the wealthy Hearst was just another capitalist. The more conservative *New York Times* at first dismissed his candidacy. Now, the paper asked Republicans to vote for the current Democratic mayor, George McClellan, in order to defeat Hearst. The New York Democratic Party, controlled by a political machine known as Tammany Hall, called Hearst a disaster for the city. Still, Hearst was popular among many Democrats.

The truth was that people did not see Hearst as a radical. He appeared at campaign events dressed

Tammany Hall

Tammany Hall was the Democratic Party's political machine, which controlled politics in New York City until the mid-1930s. If people voted for or gave money to Tammany politicians, they were rewarded with jobs, city services, or building contracts. That was how the machine worked. "Bosses" were Tammany leaders who chose political candidates, helped get out the vote, and provided rewards to loyal supporters. Tammany helped immigrants— especially the Irish—gain political power in the United States. However, the organization was mainly known for political corruption. It took bribes, gave profitable city contracts to members, and stole city money and elections. Tammany became so corrupt that the name is still used to describe corrupt politics.

The most notorious Tammany boss was William Tweed. He swindled millions of dollars from the city in the 1850s and 1860s. A series of famous political cartoons helped ruin Tweed's political career. In 1871, Tweed was arrested for corruption, and he died in jail in 1878.

A tiger usually symbolized the Tammany Hall political machine in cartoons and posters.

conservatively. He spoke softly and courteously. He said his wealth was a good reason to elect him. "I am not in this election because I have any itch for office or because I want the salary, but because I want to accomplish something for your benefit and win your approval."[1]

On the Saturday before election day, Hearst gave a series of speeches in Brooklyn and Manhattan. The Sunday before the election, pollsters were confused by Hearst's enormous strength among Democrats. City leaders worried that this third-party candidate, this notorious publisher, would actually win the election.

On Sunday night, Hearst sponsored a free concert at Madison Square Garden. When he and his wife entered the theater, Hearst got a huge ovation from the large crowd. Blocks away, Tammany Hall was holding an anti-Hearst rally. Hundreds of police kept the overflow crowd at Hearst's event from marching to confront Tammany's supporters.

The next morning, the *New York Times* made a prediction: if Hearst were elected mayor, he would run for governor in 1906 and possibly win. This prospect particularly alarmed conservatives of both parties. The governorship was seen as a step toward becoming president.

Based on preelection polls, Hearst had every reason to expect victory. He was confident, but he had been warned that Tammany Hall would do anything and everything to beat him.

A Wild Election

Hearst walked to the polls and cast his vote at 6:45 a.m. on November 7, 1905. A crowd of supporters applauded him. He then spent the rest of the day at his election headquarters. He watched with growing horror as more and more evidence of voting fraud turned up.

Witnesses and voters staggered in, covered with blood. They told stories of Tammany Hall thugs offering them bribes to vote against Hearst. They recounted how they were beaten when they refused. While his staff grew increasingly upset, Hearst remained calm. He got help for the injured and sent new people out to watch the voting.

Reports came in telling of ballot stuffing, or the illegal addition of votes to the ballot box. Witnesses described how gangs used violence against Hearst voters and how Tammany Hall paid people to vote more than once. Still, Hearst remained confident that his crusade for reform of city government would be successful.

The first election returns looked so good that the earliest *New York American* edition announced

New York Papers

Hearst published four New York City newspapers: the morning and Sunday editions of the *New York Journal* (later renamed the *American*), the *Evening Journal*, and a German-language daily called *New Yorker Morgen Journal*.

that Hearst had been elected mayor. Then, bad news came. Vote counting was delayed, ballots were disqualified, and voting boxes in precincts favoring Hearst were dumped in a river. When the official tally was announced, Hearst had narrowly lost to Democrat McClellan, with the Republican candidate a distant third.

Hearst's supporters called the election a fraud and demanded that Hearst become mayor. Fearing violence from Tammany Hall, Hearst advised against further demonstrations. He vowed to find out who stole the election. He was confident that he would get justice through a recount or legal action. He also offered a reward for the conviction of those involved in the fraud. However, none of his efforts overturned the election results. On December 27, McClellan was officially declared mayor-elect of New York City.

Hearst was not discouraged by his loss. The election had received nationwide coverage. He had done amazingly well as the candidate of a third political party. His appeal to immigrants,

"Few individuals in American history—with the exception of certain Presidents—have affected or helped shape the course of this nation's history over a fifty-year period, either favorably or wrongly, more than William Randolph Hearst."[2]
—*Ben Proctor,*
Hearst biographer

support for labor unions, and demand for reforms made him a powerful political force. After this election, Tammany Hall started nominating reform candidates. McClellan accepted Hearst's argument about city ownership of public services. Hearst's challenge led to the passage of some of New York's most important reform legislation.

Just about everyone, including Hearst's enemies, believed that Tammany Hall had stolen the election. Even the *New York Times* admitted this. But they also congratulated the city's voters for defeating Hearst, writing that "the election of Mr. HEARST to be Mayor of New York would have sent a shiver of apprehension over the entire Union."[3] Hearst continued to contest the election. However, no one in power was willing to be responsible for a Hearst victory. The political establishment was afraid of his ideas and his popular support. Hearst may have lost his bid for mayor of New York City in 1905, but his political aspirations did not end. Hearst would continue to fight for the people and make his opinions heard. As a politician and a publisher, William Randolph Hearst would soon become an undeniable force. ⌐

HEARST FOR MAYOR

MUNICIPAL LEAGUE NOMINATION

MARK YOUR BALLOT IN THE CIRCLE UNDER THE SCALES

Hearst created his own political party, the Municipal Ownership League, when he ran for mayor of New York City in 1905.

William's mother, Phoebe, wanted only the finest things in life for her son.

BOOMTOWN BOY

In the 1860s, San Francisco, California, was booming. New buildings, new ethnic populations, and new energy made it a city on the rise. People had been flocking to the region since 1848, when gold was discovered at John Sutter's sawmill in nearby Sacramento. At that time, California was not yet a state and San Francisco had only 800 residents. By 1860, San Francisco's population had reached more than 50,000. William Randolph Hearst was born in the city in 1863.

SON OF A MINER

William Randolph Hearst's father, George, was born in 1820 in Franklin County, Missouri. He tried to resist the lure of the stories of gold strikes near San Francisco. But in 1850, the eager young man left Missouri for California, joining thousands of other treasure seekers and adventurers.

George was a risk taker: courageous, single-minded, and determined to succeed. In 1859, he invested in a mine that turned out to be full of silver. George bought as many mine shares as he could. He invested his money wisely and became rich.

In 1860, ten years after he had left home, George returned to Missouri to take care of his sick mother. There, he met and married Phoebe Apperson. When they met, George was 41 years old. He was tall and strong, with a scraggly beard, rough habits and manners, and little formal education. Phoebe was a 19-year-old schoolteacher. Though small, shy, and refined, Phoebe was also an ambitious and determined young woman. She saw in George a way out of her rural Missouri life. The two were married on June 15, 1862. The couple's only child was born in San Francisco on April 29, 1863. They named him William Randolph, after his grandfathers.

For the next 20 years, George spent most of his time at his mining camps. Phoebe devoted herself entirely to "Willie." She was determined to educate her son and herself at the same time. Her Willie would be cultured and refined, she vowed. He would not be rough and unsophisticated like his father. He would learn to love music, art, and literature. He would see the world!

What William Wants

In an interview, Hearst's father observed: "There's only one thing that's sure about my boy Bill. I've been watching him and notice that when he wants cake, he wants cake, and he wants it now. And I notice that after a while he gets the cake."[1]

AN UNUSUAL EDUCATION

Young William was a bright, curious boy. He was given whatever he wanted, and he soon learned to feel as though he deserved only the best. William developed an early awareness of the power of wealth. He also had an early love of mischief, pranks, jokes, and performances. When he was an old man, Hearst wrote several newspaper columns about his childhood. He called himself "an ordinary American brat."[2] But William was far from ordinary.

William was mostly homeschooled, although he was seldom at home. In the spring of 1873, William accompanied his mother on an 18-month trip to Europe. Phoebe also took along a tutor for her son. She faithfully recorded their adventures in a diary. They toured at least a dozen countries. Although he was only ten, William enjoyed the long trip. He was keenly interested in what they saw and showed sympathy for human and animal suffering. He hated to see the overworked horses in Dublin, Ireland, and wanted to give away all he had to the poor people there.

By the time Phoebe and William headed home from their trip abroad, he had developed an interest in ancient and modern art and architecture. At ten years old, he became an ardent collector, insisting on owning everything that attracted him.

Contradictions in young William's personality were emerging. William was both shy and an eager showman and prankster. He was quiet, but he loved fireworks, noise, crowds, and sensational events. He was learning to manipulate people for his own benefit. He found ways to avoid discipline and rules. However, William was sympathetic to the less fortunate. He had an artistic eye and a quick mind.

William's childhood, while privileged, was marked by frequent changes. He faced difficulty making friends and establishing roots because he moved in and out of many schools. His mother was loving, overprotective, and demanding. His father was largely absent.

HARVARD AND THE *LAMPOON*

When William was in his mid-teens, his mother decided he must go to Harvard University, a prestigious school in Massachusetts.

George Hearst and Politics

George Hearst had close ties to the Democratic Party. In 1865, he served in the California State Assembly, but he returned to mining after one term. In 1880, he bought the *San Francisco Examiner* and quit mining to devote himself to politics. He hoped to become senator or governor. With a newspaper of his own and lots of money, George Hearst became a major political power.

In 1884, during the presidential campaign of Democrat Grover Cleveland, George ran for senator. Although Cleveland won, California voted Republican. Since state legislatures, not the voters, elected senators at that time, Republican John Miller was sent to the Senate. However, George Hearst was named to finish Miller's term when the Republican died in 1886. He was elected to the Senate in his own right in 1887. The day he took his oath of office—March 4, 1887—was the same day "W. R. Hearst, Proprietor" appeared for the first time on the masthead of the *San Francisco Examiner.*

To prepare him for college, she
enrolled William in St. Paul's
Episcopal School near Concord,
New Hampshire. Far from home and
miserable, William hated everything
about the school. He despised the
rules, the rituals, and the snobbery
of the socially elite, just as his father
did. Taking pity on him, William's
parents withdrew him after one
school year. He spent the next two years studying for
Harvard's entrance exams with tutors.

"Grandma said Pop never once expressed a regret or misgiving about Harvard. He never looked back. He had other aims and didn't like wasting time."[3]
—*William Randolph Hearst Jr., recalling his father's college years*

In the fall of 1882, William left for Harvard. At
first, he was homesick and unhappy. He coped by
generously spending his large allowance and getting
into trouble with his friends. He was 19, tall, thin,
and shy, with a high-pitched voice that embarrassed
him. He had rather startling blue-gray eyes and
a habit of looking directly and intensely at those
speaking to him. William was very intelligent and
knew his mother wanted him to succeed in school.
But he had his father's independent spirit and
tendency to not conform. He resented discipline
and loved to challenge authority. He never applied
himself to anything that did not interest him.

The high point of William's Harvard years was his first experience in publishing. He was appointed business manager of the university's humor magazine, the *Harvard Lampoon*. He quickly increased the publication's revenue from advertisements. Under Hearst's direction, the *Lampoon* went from being in debt to turning a profit.

William became notorious for his pranks and noisy parties at Harvard. He was placed on academic probation in November of his sophomore year. After his junior year, he was asked to leave the school. This did not bother him at all. He knew what he wanted to do, and his plans did not involve school.

William had developed a strong interest in journalism. This, along with his success with the *Lampoon*, prompted William to study the newspaper business. When he was supposed to be studying for his exams, William was actually studying Joseph Pulitzer's newspaper, the *New York World*. In 1880, William's father had acquired a small newspaper, the *San Francisco Examiner*. He wanted to publicize the Democratic Party and his political ambitions. William received the *Examiner* in the mail and thought it was not as good as the New York papers he read. He decided to take over his father's newspaper.

William Randolph Hearst

As a young adult, William was already interested
in the newspaper business.

Hearst improved the San Francisco Examiner *by adding large illustrations.*

Monarch of the Dailies

In late 1885, William Randolph Hearst wrote a letter to his father with specific ideas for improving the *San Francisco Examiner*. The letter showed how deeply Hearst had studied the newspaper industry and how confident he was.

He urged his father to follow the example of the *New York World*. Hearst also shared his interest in managing the *Examiner*, writing, "I am convinced that I could run a newspaper successfully."[1]

STARTING WITH A BANG

Hearst returned to San Francisco in 1887 with ambition, energy, and originality. His father had begun his political career and made young Hearst manager of the *San Francisco Examiner*. Hearst publicized his new paper with half-page ads, proclaiming the *Examiner* "Monarch of the Dailies! The Largest, Brightest and Best Newspaper on the Pacific Coast."[2] During the next eight years as he ran the paper, Hearst developed most of the attitudes, techniques, and philosophy he would maintain as a newspaperman for the rest of his life.

From the start, Hearst was a hands-on boss. He loved the action and excitement of the newsroom, getting his hands full of ink at the

A New Kind of Newspaper

When Hearst began his newspaper career in 1887, U.S. readers looked to newspapers for information and entertainment. Advances in printing and papermaking made it possible to produce a newspaper that could be sold for only one or two cents a copy. The new newspapers appealed to a wider audience and were sold on the street rather than through subscription. They used a simpler and more direct style, with vivid language and compelling human-interest stories. No longer filled with drab, narrow columns of type, these papers attracted the eye with large, bold headlines and illustrations—just as newspapers still do today.

presses and making the decisions. By and large, his staff loved him—partly because he always believed in hiring talented people and paying them well. Hearst demanded imaginative writing and dramatic presentation. He offered bonuses or salary increases for jobs well done. Hearst liked his people to receive credit for their work. He published many writers' names as bylines, which was not a common practice at the time. His newsroom was an exciting place, and his staff responded with loyalty and gratitude.

A Bold, New *Examiner*

Hearst was convinced that a newspaper had to look good to be successful. That called for the latest in printing equipment, no matter how much it cost. As he had promised his father, Hearst made the *Examiner* more attractive, starting with the front page. He reduced the number of columns and stories, doubled the size of headlines, and added line drawings that extended across several columns. He believed illustrations

Making Big Stories

Hearst was a master at making a small story huge. An early example was the *Examiner's* coverage of a fire that destroyed a hotel in Monterey, California. Hearst hired a train to carry his writers and artists to Monterey and devoted an entire 14-page edition of the paper to the fire. His enormous front-page headlines began with the words "HUNGRY, FRANTIC FLAMES," and the story featured dramatic language such as "Splendid Pleasure Palace," "Scene of Terror," and "a Smoldering Heap of Ashes."[3]

*Hearst used the most advanced printing presses
to make his newspaper look better.*

helped newly literate readers comprehend stories.
Quality pictures also attracted attention.

Critics worried that illustrated newspapers
oversimplified the real issues and focused on the
trivial. But to Hearst, a newspaper had to entertain
as well as inform. No matter what the story, he made
sure to emphasize the splendid service provided to

the people of San Francisco by his great newspaper. Hearst surpassed rival newspapers and overwhelmed the public, who loved the constant surprises.

Hearst wanted the paper to appeal to all readers. He increased sports coverage, publicized community events, and held personal interviews with prominent people. He also allowed his editorial writers the freedom to be controversial. Always good at sensing what people wanted to read, he began running crime stories on his front page. He added them until he was devoting more space to crime than to any other topic. Each story was accompanied by illustrations or cartoons.

"[*San Francisco Examiner* editor Arthur] McEwen wanted readers to say 'Gee whiz!' on seeing the front page. They were to holler 'Holy Moses!' on glancing at the second page. And by Page Three, they should leap from their seats and shout 'God a'mighty!' Somebody once said, 'San Franciscans went to a party every time they picked up the *Examiner*.'"[4]
—*William Randolph Hearst Jr.*

As time went on, the *Examiner*'s articles sounded more and more like short stories. The line between reporting and fiction was no longer clear. At the time, readers did not necessarily expect objective reporting. They liked to read exciting news. Stories could be exaggerated—or even made up—to support Hearst's social crusades. Generally, however, Hearst's newspaper was as accurate as others of the time.

Hearst knew that increased circulation led businesses to buy ads in the paper. Money from advertising was the chief source of the paper's revenue. So, Hearst promoted his newspaper on billboards and with marching bands, oyster suppers, fireworks displays, and free boat rides. He hosted celebrations, held charity drives, and invited readers to write letters to the paper.

Hearst's *Examiner*, like Pulitzer's *New York World*, was an activist newspaper. Rather than taking an objective viewpoint, as newspapers

Annie Laurie and the Sob Sisters

Hearst's most famous reporter in San Francisco was Winifred Black. Under the pen name Annie Laurie, she became a leading "sob sister"—a female feature writer known for her emotional prose. One of Black's first assignments was typical of Hearst's two passions: increasing readership and exposing corruption and injustice. She disguised herself as a poor, sick, demented street person and was admitted to the City Receiving Hospital. There, she observed what had been rumored: the hospital neglected poor patients or treated them cruelly. Her story in the *Examiner* led to public outrage and the removal of most of the hospital staff. Such stunts were often examples of solid investigative journalism. They were splashy and colorful, but they succeeded in using the power of the press to expose injustices, corruption, and incompetence.

Journalism was one of the first traditionally male professions to welcome women. Over the next few years, Black carried out a series of undercover investigations that exposed political corruption and government inefficiency. She also reported on the floods in Galveston, Texas, the San Francisco earthquake, and the Versailles Peace Conference after World War I. When Hearst eventually moved to New York, Black followed to write for his papers there.

attempt to do today, the *Examiner* was passionately on the side of working people, labor unions, and the right to strike. Although he refused to let the *Examiner* be a tool of any political party, Hearst was dedicated to progressive causes. He was determined to expose police and government corruption and negligence. The *Examiner* campaigned on its front pages for better streets, schools, and teachers. Over the years, some of Hearst's crusades brought results, and some did not. All helped to establish Hearst in the public mind as a champion of the people. And they brought him the devoted readership of immigrants and the working class. Within his first year of managing the *Examiner*, circulation doubled.

Hearst's father died in 1891, leaving everything to his wife and nothing to his son. Without control of the family fortune, Hearst had to rely on his mother to finance his business moves. Still, five months after his father's death, Hearst started looking for a New York newspaper to buy. He wanted to take on Pulitzer.

This cartoon appeared in a Hearst newspaper in 1901.
It shows how big business treated workers badly.

*Joseph Pulitzer was Hearst's chief rival in
New York City's newspaper industry.*

Newspaper Wars

When William Randolph Hearst took on New York City in 1895, he was entering a competitive field. New York already had more than a dozen major daily newspapers. The city had 3 million potential readers in its ethnically and economically diverse population. Of the nine morning papers, Joseph Pulitzer's *New York World* was the most famous and had the largest circulation. Hearst bought the *New York Morning Journal* and its German-language version at a bargain price. Despite the odds, he was optimistic and confident, as always.

A WINNING STRATEGY

Hearst quickly put together an excellent staff. He also shortened the name of the paper to the *New York Journal*. He decided to charge a penny per copy—but he would give readers as much news and entertainment as Pulitzer was for two cents. In the first issue, Hearst showed New Yorkers what they could expect by turning what had been a dull, insignificant newspaper into a sensation. The slogan on his masthead read, "You can't get more than all the news. You can't pay less than one cent."[1]

New York readers soon became accustomed to Hearst's trademark huge headlines, dramatic writing, spectacular illustrations and cartoons, and nonstop publicity. They also found excellent reporting and analysis. Always a superb salesman, Hearst advertised his paper on billboards all over the city.

SHARPENED POLITICAL FOCUS

Hearst intended to make the *Journal* a popular and progressive daily. He needed to establish himself in New York as a champion of the working class. Like Pulitzer's *World*, Hearst's *Journal* was prolabor, pro-immigrant, and anti-big business. Hearst was not yet interested in running for office, but he was a loyal Democrat who attacked the Republican Party relentlessly as the party of wealth and privilege.

The *Journal* launched hundreds of crusades and reported regularly on its own investigations and triumphs. Hearst campaigned for public ownership of utilities—gas, water, and ice—and fairer taxation. Hearst also helped collect blankets for poor people, raise money for needy families, and organize funds for striking workers. To Hearst, this was the "new journalism" in which newspapers were active participants

Joseph Pulitzer

Joseph Pulitzer was a Hungarian immigrant. He became a leading newspaperman in St. Louis, Missouri. He published articles that championed working people and immigrants. When he purchased the *New York World* in 1883, Pulitzer changed its focus to stories about ordinary people, exciting scandals, and shocking exposés of government corruption and police incompetence.

Pulitzer published many sensational stories, but he also believed that newspapers were public institutions with a duty to improve society. He put the *World* in the service of social reform and developed strong ties to the Democratic Party. Pulitzer realized newspapers had great power to influence public opinion.

in community affairs. By the end of his first year as owner, the *Journal* was the most colorful activist newspaper in the city. In 1896, Hearst started the *Evening Journal* to compete with Pulitzer's *Evening World*. Now, he had several editions: morning, evening, German, and Sunday.

SUCCESS ON SUNDAY

The most profitable element in newspaper publishing was the Sunday paper. Similar to a weekly magazine, it was packed with special features and advertising. Hearst intended to compete with Pulitzer's successful Sunday edition. He made unbeatable salary offers to Pulitzer's employees, which they all accepted, including the Sunday editor.

The *Journal*'s big Sunday paper cost five cents. Hearst included several full-color supplements. The most popular and profitable of these was the *American Humorist*, which featured

Leaving Pulitzer for Hearst

Hearst lured away Pulitzer's editors, reporters, and artists with more money. However, financial gain was not their only motive. Pulitzer had also become a difficult man to work with. Blind and sickly, Pulitzer no longer could manage his papers personally, but he continued to interfere with his editors and business managers. He was forever moving people from job to job and changing their responsibilities, creating chaos in his offices. In contrast, Hearst offered job security. His staff signed multiyear contracts—a first in the newspaper business. He also encouraged bylines, which identified writers by name.

This 1898 poster advertised Hearst's Sunday paper.

color comics. Hearst loved comics and supported them enthusiastically throughout his career.

Pulitzer tried to compete with Hearst. He dropped the price of the *World* to one cent, believing no reader would choose Hearst's upstart *Journal* if

both papers cost the same. But Pulitzer was wrong.
Hearst continued to pour money into his newspaper,
and Pulitzer's new staff continued to move to Hearst.
In 1897, Hearst hired Arthur Brisbane. At the *World*,
Brisbane had been the replacement for Pulitzer's
last Sunday editor, who had already been hired by
Hearst. Brisbane became one of Hearst's closest
associates.

As the nineteenth century came to a close, a war
with Spain would bring Hearst and Pulitzer's rivalry
to a head.

THE SPANISH-AMERICAN WAR

The island of Cuba lies 90 miles (145 km) off
the coast of Florida. At the end of the nineteenth
century, Cuba was ruled by Spain. Periodically,
Cuban rebels fought against Spanish rule. In
early 1896, Spain sent 150,000 troops to Cuba
and forced tens of thousands of Cubans into
"reconcentration" camps to prevent them from
helping or joining the rebels. Thousands died of
disease and starvation.

Hearst believed that Spanish oppression of the
Cubans was wrong. Spain had no right to maintain
a colonial empire so close to the United States,

Comics Pioneer

Hearst was a devoted fan and loyal reader of comics. He also appreciated comics because they increased newspaper subscriptions. In 1897, Hearst asked cartoonist Rudolph Dirks to create two mischievous boys similar to those he remembered from the German comic books he had read as a boy. The *Katzenjammer Kids*, the oldest comic strip still in syndication, was the first comic to use sequential narrative panels with speech balloons.

In coming years, Hearst added other comic strips with continuing characters. In 1912, the *Journal* introduced the first full page of comics on weekdays. Hearst's comics were among the first to be reprinted in booklets, leading to modern comic books. In 1916, Hearst's International Film Service became a pioneering animation studio using characters from Hearst's newspaper strips.

and its presence was a threat to U.S. interests. The situation in Cuba provided the perfect scenario for screaming headlines and melodramatic storytelling—and for boosting readership.

The *Journal* kept the situation on its front page, even when events temporarily cooled down. Meanwhile, Pulitzer's *World* struggled to keep up. Both papers published any anti-Spanish stories they received, regardless of origin or authenticity. Getting all their information from the rebels, the papers plastered their front pages with stories and pictures of Spain's brutality. This type of writing, in which newspapers print sensational stories without regard to the truth in order to change public opinion or sell papers, is known as "yellow journalism."

In early 1897, Hearst sent reporter Richard Harding Davis

and artist Frederick Remington to cover the story in Cuba. Davis wrote a few dramatic stories on the suffering he saw. Remington, however, could not find anything worth illustrating. According to one popular story, Remington sent a telegram to Hearst about returning to New York because there was no war. Supposedly, Hearst cabled back, "Please remain. You furnish the pictures, and I'll furnish the war."[2]

Hearst denied writing the telegram. The incident was mentioned once in

Yellow Journalism

One of Pulitzer's most popular cartoonists was Richard Outcault. His cartoon series centered on a bald, big-eared, buck-toothed immigrant boy in a yellow nightshirt known as the Yellow Kid. In fall 1896, Hearst hired Outcault. Pulitzer tried to compete by hiring another cartoonist to draw his own Yellow Kid. For a while, New York had two Yellow Kids every Sunday. This competition made the *World* and the *Journal* widely known as "The Yellow Kid Papers." This was shortened to "The Yellow Papers," or "The Yellows," which then became "yellow journalism." Today, yellow journalism is a negative term to describe newspapers that use unethical or sensational practices to sell copies.

Ervin Wardman, editor of the conservative *New York Press*, was the first to use the term yellow journalism to describe Hearst and Pulitzer. He hated the Yellow Kid cartoons. He was condemning the *Journal* and the *World* for bad taste more than anything else. The term later grew to include unethical action, not just poor taste. Many aspects of so-called yellow journalism became a permanent feature of popular newspapers in the United States and Europe during the twentieth century. These included banner headlines, sensational stories, an emphasis on illustrations, and colored supplements.

The term "yellow journalism" came from
this cartoon character, the Yellow Kid.

the memoirs of a close Hearst associate. The story,
true or not, has been used ever since to condemn
Hearst for inflaming war fever to sell newspapers.
But the war was not Hearst's creation. Hearst's
and Pulitzer's newspaper coverage both stirred and
reflected U.S. excitement about what seemed a
righteous and easily won conflict.

WAR REPORTER

In 1898, the United States made the decision to intervene in Cuba. The USS *Maine* had exploded in the harbor in Havana, Cuba, and the United States blamed the Spanish. Going to war proved popular, in large part because of the sensational stories Hearst had been running.

Hearst put himself and his newspapers in the center of the war. He sent twice as many boats to cover the action as any other member of the press. Some had movie cameras set up on deck to film scenes on sea and shore.

But Hearst wanted more. Like future president Theodore Roosevelt, then assistant secretary of the navy, Hearst wanted to participate in the war he had promoted. Turned down by the army and the navy, Hearst decided to go to Cuba on his own as a war correspondent. He took this role seriously, writing a series of clear, detailed reports on the situation. Hearst traveled the battlefields believing that his readers deserved his eyewitness news gathering. He remained in Cuba for more than a month.

Hearst's efforts paid off. When he had taken over the *Journal* and its German edition in 1895, their combined sales were less than 100,000.

At the height of the Spanish-American War, single-day sales reached a high of 2.7 million copies. And yet Hearst's success was bittersweet. Hearst had defeated Pulitzer in readership, but his newspapers were losing money. He had spent vast sums on the war. He also funded a flurry of publicity and celebrations for returning U.S. troops.

Also, Hearst was restless. Since his Harvard days, Hearst had told close friends that he intended to combine careers in journalism and politics. He was convinced that he spoke for the people. Now, he was ready to run for office.

But the public did not appear ready to elect him. Roosevelt came back from the war a hero and was drafted by the Republicans to run for governor of New York. Hearst's experience was different. No parades welcomed him back. The Democrats did not ask him to run for governor. Nevertheless, Hearst was determined to pursue public office, with the presidency as his ultimate goal.

*William Randolph Hearst took photographs in Cuba
during the Spanish-American War.*

COPYRIGHT 1906
BY ALVA E. STERN.

.THE TRUSTS

HEARST IN WAR.

HEARST IN PEACE.

HEARST IN THE HEARTS
OF HIS COUNTRYMEN.

This postcard advertises Hearst's bid for governor of New York in 1906.

RUNNING FOR OFFICE

Despite all he had accomplished in San Francisco and New York, William Randolph Hearst wanted the power of a political office. In the years before radio, daily newspapers were the main source for political news. As Hearst was well aware, newspaper publishers greatly influenced voters. Since his earliest days at the *San Francisco Examiner*, Hearst had used his newspapers to crusade for social and political reforms—and for the politicians who supported them.

Once Hearst decided to run for public office, he used his newspapers to vigorously promote his platform and issues. Before he was a candidate, Hearst was a hands-on newspaperman. After he began campaigning for office, he largely left the day-to-day publishing work to his staff. However, he continued to maintain absolute control over the opinions expressed in his newspapers.

Government by Newspaper

Hearst became heavily involved in politics in 1898, when Theodore Roosevelt ran for governor of New York. Hearst organized a newspaper campaign ridiculing Roosevelt in fierce political cartoons and editorials. Roosevelt won the election, but Hearst was not discouraged. Although he had never held an elected office, Hearst decided to position himself to run for vice president in 1900. Popular speaker Williams Jennings Bryan was the front-runner Democratic presidential candidate. Bryan had also run against President William McKinley in 1896.

Hearst made sure his own name appeared all over his newspapers by writing editorials on every significant foreign and domestic issue. Still an outsider in the Democratic Party, Hearst realized he needed a national voice that extended beyond New York and San Francisco. Fortunately, in April 1900, Bryan's allies asked Hearst to start a newspaper in Chicago, Illinois. Bryan was weak in the Midwest, and Chicago's newspapers were mostly Republican. Working with impressive speed, Hearst had the first issue of the *Chicago American* ready by July 4, 1900.

Despite Hearst's efforts, the Democratic Party did not choose him to run with Bryan. Instead, Hearst took the presidency of the National Association of Democratic Clubs, an organization that produced campaign literature. Democratic leaders hoped

Radical Endorsement

Democrat William Jennings Bryan faced Republican William McKinley for the first time in the election of 1896. Hearst's *Journal* was the only New York paper to endorse Bryan. Mainstream Democrats considered Bryan too radical. Although Bryan lost, Hearst had strengthened his progressive reputation and won many readers away from Pulitzer, who, for the first time, had declined to support a Democratic candidate.

the association would serve as a network of grassroots organizations furnishing campaign volunteers. Hearst, however, inflated its importance and his own by holding rallies and behaving like a prominent Democrat.

President William McKinley, a Republican, won reelection in November. Though the Democrats had lost the presidential election, Hearst increased his own national visibility.

A MISTAKE

Next, Hearst made a costly mistake. President McKinley was assassinated in 1901. Earlier in the year, when the governor-elect of Kentucky had been killed in an election dispute, the *Journal* published a poem by Ambrose Bierce that seemed to predict McKinley's murder. In April 1901, just before McKinley's second inauguration,

Boss Hanna

During the presidential election of 1896, cartoonist Homer Davenport developed a famous caricature of Mark Hanna, McKinley's manager and a prominent Democratic boss. The *Journal's* front page carried a daily Davenport cartoon that showed a bloated "Boss Hanna" covered by dollar signs and with his puppet McKinley.

William McKinley speaking to a crowd in 1900

an editorial claimed political assassinations were sometimes necessary. Hearst was held responsible for creating a political climate that led to violence. The backlash against him included death threats, newspaper boycotts, and accusations of murder.

To fight negative publicity and emphasize his patriotism, Hearst renamed the morning edition of the *Journal*, calling it the *New York American*. He left politics for a while to concentrate on his publishing empire. In 1902, he added a second Chicago newspaper.

Congressman Hearst

Hearst returned to New York politics in 1902. He wanted to run for governor, but the Democrats never seriously considered him. They needed his money and influence, however, so they nominated Hearst for a vacant seat in the U.S. House of Representatives. When he was elected, he proclaimed himself the champion of the country's working people and immigrants.

Hearst began to prepare for the 1904 presidential election. To reach more potential voters, he bought a newspaper in Los Angeles, California, and another in Boston, Massachusetts. Through the summer and fall of 1903, Hearst's publications built up his campaign.

Hearst officially announced his candidacy in January 1904.

Loyal to Bierce

Because of his biting social criticism and satire, Ambrose Bierce had a controversial newspaper career. His poem about the governor-elect of Kentucky was meant to express a fearful national mood. Instead, it stirred up a storm of hostile reaction against Hearst. Although the uproar helped end Hearst's chances for the presidency, Hearst never revealed who wrote the poem. He also never fired Bierce.

Organized labor backed the publisher because of his unwavering support for the unions. Finally forced to take his political ambitions seriously, Hearst's critics began making vicious attacks on his character and morals. The *New York Evening Post* published an editorial called "The Unthinkable Hearst."[1]

Cosmopolitan Magazine

In the midst of his political activities, Hearst continued to expand his publishing empire. In 1905, he bought *Cosmopolitan* magazine, then a general-interest monthly that specialized in exposing political corruption. Beginning in March 1906, the magazine featured an attack on corruption in Washington DC. Publicized in Hearst's newspapers, the article helped increase *Cosmopolitan*'s circulation by 50 percent. The article was part of a growing movement of journalism that sought to expose problems in society. Not long after the article was published, President Roosevelt coined the term "muckraking" for the kind of investigative journalism that focused too much, in his opinion, on the negative aspects of society. The term was soon proudly adopted by many investigative journalists.

Social-activist writers such as Ambrose Bierce, Jack London, and Upton Sinclair all wrote for the magazine. Though its focus has changed to fashion and women's issues, *Cosmopolitan* is still published by Hearst Magazines. Today, it is one of the best-selling magazines in the world.

At the Democratic National Convention in St. Louis, Missouri, Hearst's name was considered for nomination. But as expected, the party nominated Alton Parker, the favorite of its conservative wing. Exhausted, Hearst was reelected to Congress without campaigning. His papers endorsed Parker, but they did not rally for him. Parker lost to Theodore Roosevelt in 1904 by a huge margin.

From Governor to President?

In 1905, Hearst formed a new political party, the Municipal Ownership League, and ran for mayor of New York. He lost, but he did extremely well and received a lot of national publicity. Afterward, Hearst decided to run for governor in 1906 as a path to the White House, and he made successful speeches all over the state. He used "talking pictures," filming his speeches and showing the films to voters living outside New York City. He made sure his message was everywhere.

A week before the election, President Roosevelt sent Secretary of State Elihu Root to New York to speak against Hearst. Calling Hearst "an insincere, self-seeking demagogue,"[2] Root reminded voters that Roosevelt considered Hearst partly responsible for McKinley's assassination. Hearst tried to defend himself, but the attack came too close to the election, and he lost. Hearst was not ready to give up, though. He was convinced more than ever that both major parties were corrupt. He worked to transform his Municipal Ownership League, renamed the Independence League, into a national force. However, Hearst was never elected to another office, and his political party did not remain active past 1914.

ONCE MORE A CANDIDATE

Hearst announced in October 1909 that he was running for mayor again on his third-party ticket. However, the Tammany Hall Democrats nominated a well-known reformer who competed with Hearst on his trademark issues. In a vicious campaign, Hearst smeared the Democrat candidate while Tammany Hall assaulted Hearst's character.

Hearst lost the election by a wide margin, but that did not slow his momentum. The next year, he ran for lieutenant governor of New York for his political party and lost. His political career had peaked and was on the decline, though he was not yet willing to accept the fact. Hearst perhaps realized that his Independence League party was getting him nowhere. In fall 1911, Hearst announced that he was again a member of the Democratic Party in order to have a say in the party's nominee for the 1912 election.

Theodore Roosevelt became president when
William McKinley was assassinated.

*Newspapers were widely read at the beginning of the twentieth century.
Hearst's many papers could influence public opinion.*

QUESTIONS OF LOYALTY

William Randolph Hearst had failed to become mayor or governor—much less president of the United States. Still, he was not going to give up his mission of trumpeting the people's voice. Though his politics would change as he grew older, his belief in "government by newspaper" never wavered. Nor had Hearst given up all hope of the presidency. He certainly intended to help the Democratic Party select a presidential nominee in 1912. When the Democrats ignored his published criticisms, Hearst decided that he needed to add publications and organize his media empire to continue to shape public opinion.

EMPIRE BUILDING

In 1909, Hearst had formed the International News Service (INS) to coordinate the sharing of information and stories among his newspapers. In 1912, Hearst added a Southern newspaper, the *Atlanta Georgian.* Now, he had newspapers in every region of the country and in six of the largest cities: San Francisco, New York, Chicago, Los Angeles, Boston, and Atlanta. He had also added to his magazine empire with *Good Housekeeping*, *World Today* (renamed *Hearst's Magazine*), and *Harper's Bazaar.* To organize and manage his print media, Hearst believed in syndication—sharing news, editorials, features, photographs, and the Sunday comics among his various publications. He had also begun to sell these items to subscribers in cities without Hearst

Daily Scrutiny

Edmond Coblentz, an associate of Hearst for more than 50 years, recalled Hearst's deep knowledge of all aspects of the newspaper business. Even after Hearst began managing his newspapers from afar, they all "came under his daily scrutiny, and never a day passed that some one of his lieutenants did not receive a word of praise, criticism, or suggestion for change."[1]

newspapers. In 1915, he formed a separate features service called King Feature Service. Syndication was a relatively new idea then, and Hearst embraced it enthusiastically.

In 1914 and 1915, Hearst took steps to ensure that all his publications operated more closely under his direction. He instructed his editors to support issues he endorsed, provide more accurate stories, cover a wider variety of interests, and concentrate on superior photography. Hearst insisted on being consulted in advance about all important stories and features. His staff called him "the Chief."

Hearst's *New York American* had the largest circulation of any newspaper in the United States. Hearst continued to support an outstanding staff of journalists, photographers, and artists, some of whom had been with him for years. The paper featured excellently illustrated articles on topics such as politics, entertainment, New York high society, books, sports, and business. With no competition yet from radio and television, the big *Sunday New York*

American provided a week's worth of information, education, and amusement for the entire family.

Hearst was also ready to embrace the new medium of motion pictures. He was already using elements of his publications for short, filmed news stories called newsreels. He used news stories for newsreels, Sunday comics for animated cartoons, and episodes of serial films in his Sunday supplements. The next step was to adapt stories he published into full-length feature films and publicize the films in his newspapers and magazines. Hearst was a pioneer in combining his various enterprises for the greater profit of his

The Perils of Pauline

Hearst opened a New York studio, Hearst International Films, to create films and serials based on stories from his magazines and Sunday papers. On March 31, 1914, *The Perils of Pauline*, a silent film, premiered in New York theaters. Mostly written by Hearst, this serial of 20 episodes starred a young actress who specialized in hazardous escapes from villains. At the end of an episode, she was often left hanging off a cliff. This series inspired the word *cliffhanger* to describe an ending that leaves the character in danger or the plot unresolved.

The day before each episode appeared in theaters, Hearst papers carried the illustrated story of that episode as a Sunday feature. By 1915, Hearst was also supplying cartoons, or animated films, starring his most popular Sunday comics characters. Soon, the Hearst name appeared regularly on the nation's movie screens. All Hearst productions got free publicity in Hearst newspapers and were praised by Hearst newspapers' movie reviewers. Those rave reviews were then recycled into ads for other publications.

communications empire. His newspapers told dramatic, well-illustrated stories that people wanted to read. He saw the same potential in movies.

EUROPE GOES TO WAR

In the summer of 1914, World War I broke out in Europe. Soon, the Allied Powers of Great Britain and France lined up against the Central Powers of Germany and Austria-Hungary. Hearst immediately began a campaign to keep the United States out of the conflict. Convinced that all reasonable people must agree with him, he wrote to the publishers of London's two largest papers, asking them to join with him in a newspaper crusade to stop the conflict. He published the letter on his own front pages on September 10, 1914:

> *I think the press can appeal to the people, to your people, to our people and to all other people, as no other influence can. I believe that if the appeal is made now to the press of all nations, and by the press of all nations, the war can be stopped and will be stopped.*[2]

When he got no answer from London, Hearst organized his own peace offensive with huge rallies in San Francisco, Chicago, and New York. His efforts helped gain support for President Woodrow Wilson's policy of strict neutrality, but it did not affect the conflict in Europe. At the beginning of the war, many U.S citizens agreed that the United States should not get involved in the conflict in Europe. As the war went on, Hearst continued to warn his readers of the dangers of U.S. involvement. For almost a year, he led a newspaper crusade for a "League of Neutral Nations."[3] Yet, the country was growing increasingly sympathetic to the Allied Powers. Still, Hearst never wavered in his position and, as his supporters dropped, he lost money.

"The only obligation of our American institutions is to our American people, and it is our firm policy and fixed purpose to print not the things which the English government desires printed in this country but the things which the American people require for their accurate information and patriotic guidance."[5]
—*William Randolph Hearst, 1916*

As time passed, Hearst's supportive readers mainly consisted of immigrants, particularly German and Irish groups who disliked the British. Others saw Hearst as pro-German, unpatriotic, and a traitor. There were boycotts, protest meetings, and public burnings of Hearst newspapers. He became, perhaps, "the most hated man in America," but he did not back down.[4] He insisted that the papers' stance was pro-American, not pro-German or anti-British.

The New York Journal *announces U.S. entry into World War I.*

The British government banned Hearst's syndicate, International News Service, from using its cables or mail to transmit reports. France and Canada soon followed. Hearst loudly condemned what he called an attack on freedom of the press.

German officials, however, were happy to supply Hearst with stories and newsreels. Hearst did not know that several of his associates were spies for the German government. In addition, the U.S. Navy was secretly forwarding all his reports from Germany to U.S. military intelligence. Though Hearst published some material that was anti-German and pro-English, the public increasingly believed he was unpatriotic. Hearst insisted he was always and only pro-United States.

As the United States drew closer to entering the war and most U.S. citizens strongly supported the Allies, Hearst was urged by his staff to protect himself against charges of disloyalty. He bordered his pages with U.S. flags and printed some headlines in red, white, and blue. He also ran verses from the national anthem across the top of his editorial pages.

The U.S. Enters the War

After the United States declared war on Germany on April 6, 1917, Hearst directed his publications to focus on a speedy victory. He crusaded for mandatory service in the military, and his newspapers actively recruited soldiers. Hearst's papers praised the government in editorials and cartoons, although Hearst opposed any wartime attempts to quiet the press. He published testimonials from other newspapers about his own loyalty and agreed to discontinue his New York German-language newspaper until after the war. However, popular sentiment was against him.

Family Complications

In 1903, Hearst married Millicent Willson, an entertainer 19 years his junior. They had five sons in the next twelve years: George, William Randolph Jr., John, Randolph, and David. In 1915, when Hearst was 52 years old, they had the twins, Randolph and David. At this point in their marriage, however, the couple had grown less compatible. She liked high society, high style, and fancy parties. He liked the theater and nightclubs.

Not long after the twins were born, Hearst began to court Marion Davies, an 18-year-old musical-theater performer. He promoted her career in the theater pages of the *American* and the Sunday drama sections of all his papers. Though Hearst and his wife never legally divorced, Marion Davies became his companion and stayed with Hearst until his death.

Hearst's papers were still being boycotted. Hearst laughed off the attacks. But his newspapers lost money for a time. Hearst was perhaps lucky compared to others. Across the country, people who spoke out against the war were sometimes quieted by the government or attacked by prowar groups.

As it became clear that the Allies would win the war, anti-German—and anti-Hearst—feelings subsided. The public resumed buying Hearst's newspapers, mainly because they were the most attractive, best written, and most entertaining. In the years following the war, daily circulation of the *American* exceeded 1 million, and the *San Francisco Examiner* had 30 percent more advertising than its closest competitor. Hearst's success was his victory. ⌐

Hearst poses with his wife, Millicent, and their young children.

Hearst, center, standing with his political allies in New York City

NEW AND OLD ALLIANCES

William Randolph Hearst felt the Treaty of Versailles, the agreement that ended World War I, confirmed that the war should never have happened. In a signed front-page editorial, Hearst spoke out vigorously against the treaty, which he believed made another war inevitable. He was especially opposed to the part President Woodrow Wilson strongly supported: a League of Nations that would require its members to defend one another if attacked. Hearst believed this would drag the country into future conflicts.

Hearst launched a nearly two-year media crusade to turn U.S. opinion against the League of Nations. With his millions of readers, he had a powerful influence on public opinion. His influence may have had an effect on Congress, which decided to reject the treaty and the League of Nations. As a biographer of Hearst explained, "He was unalterably opposed to American involvement in European affairs and would be for the next thirty years."[1]

Hearst was so opposed to Wilson's League of Nations that, for the first time in his life, Hearst endorsed a Republican presidential candidate, Warren G. Harding, in 1920. He was delighted by Harding's landslide victory and happily proclaimed the death of the League of Nations.

CHANGING FORTUNES

In April 1919, Hearst's mother died. She left him ranches in Mexico and California and almost

"Making pictures is fundamentally like making publications. It is in each case an endeavor to entertain and interest, enlighten and uplift the public. . . . If a man knows good material and knows the public, all he has to learn is the technique of either profession."[2]
—*William Randolph Hearst*

$10 million. With his typical energy, the almost 56-year-old Hearst used his new fortune to propel his career in the film business. He established his own film studio in New York City called Cosmopolitan Productions. The company eventually moved to California and merged first with Metro-Goldwyn and then with Warner Brothers, two prominent film studios. Publicists at Cosmopolitan wrote stories about Hearst films for publication in Hearst newspapers and full-page ads.

The year 1919 also marked Hearst's first meetings with architect Julia Morgan about designing the houses, gardens, and pools on the site of his family's huge California ranch near the village of San Simeon. This spectacular project would become known as Hearst Castle.

At the time Hearst was beginning San Simeon and his business, the country's economy was in turmoil from the postwar depression and a succession of strikes. But by 1922, the economic boom under President Harding had started. Taxes were lowered for the rich, and Hearst went on a newspaper-buying spree. By 1928, he owned 28 newspapers in 19 cities.

SPREADING HIS INFLUENCE

Hearst still believed in publishing as a calling as well as a business. Increased circulation was only meaningful if people's lives were improved. He cared about the public service he believed he was providing with his political coverage, editorials, and cartoons.

With only slight exaggeration, Hearst claimed in 1924 that one of

Hearst Castle

On his hill above the Pacific Ocean in California, Hearst and famed architect and civil engineer Julia Morgan planned and built a Spanish-inspired hill town. It consisted of a half-moon of three guesthouses and a large main house, Casa Grande. The main house was topped with two towers modeled after a Spanish cathedral. Hearst and Morgan added acres of gardens, indoor and outdoor swimming pools, tennis courts, a movie theater, an airfield, and the world's largest private zoo. The complex became a home, a vacation spot for the world's most famous people, and a treasure house of world art.

Since his first childhood trip to Europe with his mother, Hearst had always collected art. Now he furnished the estate with truckloads of art and antiques bought in Europe and Egypt. He transported ornately carved ceilings, parts of European castles, and an entire Spanish monastery stone by stone.

Hearst immersed himself in the smallest details of the project and could never stop tinkering with the place. Construction paused during the Great Depression but did not stop until 1947, when Hearst moved from the estate to be closer to his doctors in Los Angeles. After his death in 1951, the Hearst Corporation donated the estate to the state of California. The Hearst San Simeon State Historical Monument opened to the public in 1958.

Hearst began building Hearst Castle in 1919.

every four families in the United States read a Hearst publication. Millions more read his syndicated features in local newspapers. Greater circulation led to more advertising and increased profits. This enabled him to offer high salaries to top journalists and artists. And he continued to be an innovator. In 1928, he added a "March of Events" section to his Sunday papers in which noted writers addressed world issues. Hearst was not the first to print such columns, but he was the first to create a Sunday section featuring them.

By 1928, he had his own California radio service. He used radio to promote his publications and his politics. His newspaper executives were slow to see radio's potential, but Hearst reminded them that their children were already radio fans. He intended to find new readers by publicizing his newspapers on Hearst-affiliated radio stations all over the country. As he reminded his staff, "It is an effort to read a newspaper; it is no effort to listen to a radio."[3]

EVER THE CRUSADER

Hearst continued to use his newspapers to promote causes that would improve his readers' lives, such as labor reforms and crusades against big business. Hearst still stayed involved in New York politics. He repeatedly proposed his name as the Democratic candidate for governor and senator. He had not entirely given up the idea of becoming president, either. Hearst's philosophy was that "citizens must abandon partisanship and blind faith in party platforms. . . . The hope for

Absent Father

Hearst and his wife, Millicent, led separate lives. Hearst spent his time with Marion Davies, an actress his media empire had made a big star. Hearst was an absent father just as his own father had been. He also interfered at a distance in his sons' lives even when they were adults, as his mother had done with him. Hearst wanted to groom them to take over his publishing empire, so he apprenticed them all to executives in his companies.

the future . . . is not in parties or in platforms, but in men."[4] City politicians considered him a threat. They understood that voters turned to newspapers for their political news, and that Hearst had substantial control of those newspapers.

The enormous growth of Hearst's publishing empire in the 1920s led to enormous debt. This, in turn, led to a shift in Hearst's editorial policies against big business. Now that he depended on bankers for loans, he did not want to offend them through his publications. Hearst, however, had long believed that his interests and the country's interests were the same. Since the flow of money from bankers was good for Hearst's business, he believed it was also good for the country. Similarly, if Republican economic policies benefited his empire's growth, then those policies were worthy of support. Hearst strongly supported the probusiness secretary of the treasury, Andrew Mellon. During Mellon's 12 years in office, Hearst's did not support Democratic presidential candidates.

BETWEEN CRUSADES

Hearst moved into Casa Grande, the main house at Hearst Castle, in 1925. Soon, he moved his business headquarters there. Hearst was comfortable in California. Movie people did not care about yellow journalism, his various feuds, his former opposition to the war, or the accusations of treason made against him. In California, Hearst controlled the major news outlets.

During the 1920s, Hearst was fairly content with the national government. He approved of President Calvin Coolidge and Secretary of the Treasury Andrew Mellon. But Hearst was only between crusades. He disapproved of the Republican administration's foreign policy. He also disliked international economic agreements and any treaties that tied U.S. prosperity to Europe. He strongly opposed U.S. participation in the World Court, which was part of the League of Nations.

Hearst believed the United States should isolate itself from Europe, and many people in the 1920s agreed with him. However, he often called for the United States to intervene in North America and South America—

Ideals versus Reality

Hearst's progressive convictions wavered a bit when he needed money. By the summer of 1923, his New York accounts were so overdrawn that bankers refused to loan him more money. Hearst then turned to a San Francisco banker. Hearst's newspapers had been attacking this banker for opposing city ownership of water and power. Hearst had campaigned a long time for city ownership of services. Now, he directed his staff to tone down their attacks.

as he had during the Spanish-American War—and in Asia, which he believed was the country's greatest potential threat. At various times, he tried to inflame public opinion against Mexico.

Hearst used his newspapers to oppose any politician who disagreed with him. But he had stopped crusading on behalf of the working class and immigrants. Instead, he tried to maintain their support by hiring various ethnic writers to supply columns.

In 1928, Hearst endorsed the Republican candidate for president, Herbert Hoover, rather than Democrat Al Smith. However, when Hoover urged U.S. participation in the World Court, Hearst went on the attack. He used his newspapers, newsreels, and radio stations to combat the idea. After Hoover was elected, the new president gave up the idea, believing the proposal had no chance.

On October 24, 1929, the stock market crashed and the United States soon entered the Great Depression. Hearst's fortunes were not affected much at first. His money was in his publications, houses, land, and art. Eventually, though, his fortunes would take a dramatic downturn.

Hearst spent his time with movie star Marion Davies.

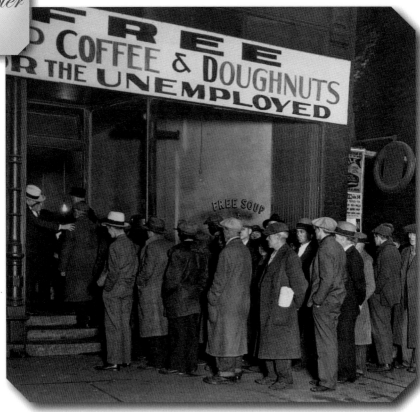

Hearst opened breadlines in New York City similar to this one in order to help people during the Depression.

TRIALS OF THE THIRTIES

With his customary optimism, William Randolph Hearst refused at first to believe that the Great Depression was a disaster without an easy solution. On November 15, 1929, the front page of all his papers featured Hearst's suggestions for restoring the economy. However, the publishing giant would not be immune to the effects of the Depression.

A Certain Sameness

Hearst had always used his papers to promote his opinions and agenda. In early 1931, he decided to add a new feature to appeal to more sophisticated readers. The result was a contributors' page written by guest authors. Hearst offered contracts to many distinguished writers, allowing them to choose their own topics. The contributors' page later became known as the op-ed because it ran opposite the editorial page. Staff editorial writers were still required to express Hearst's opinions only.

Furthermore, Hearst required his newspapers to buy and publish Hearst-syndicated material. That did not leave much space or budget for local editors to print their own material. As a result, Hearst newspapers throughout the country looked very similar and lacked local news reporting. However, this weakness was balanced by the strength of Hearst's syndicated columnists, including Damon Runyon, Walter Winchell, Robert Ripley, and Louella Parsons.

TIME TO REPLACE HOOVER

The Depression got worse. Hearst operated the two biggest breadlines in New York City, serving meals to thousands of destitute people. Instead of criticizing President Herbert Hoover's economic policies, Hearst published his own plan for recovery. He proposed that the government spend $5 billion to create jobs for the unemployed.

When Hoover ignored him, Hearst began attacking the administration. He was particularly concerned about what he saw as the president's undue interest in European affairs. In 1932, the progressive wing of the Democratic Party favored New York Governor Franklin Delano Roosevelt as its candidate in the upcoming presidential election. Hearst helped Roosevelt win the nomination.

Hearst took full credit for Roosevelt's nomination and enlisted his entire media empire to campaign for the nominee. When Roosevelt won in a landslide, Hearst was overjoyed to be a prominent Democrat again. Even before Roosevelt was sworn

"It is about time that the Democratic party got back upon the high road of Americanism. . . . Unless we American citizens are willing to go on laboring indefinitely merely to provide loot for Europe, we should personally see to it, all of us, that a man is elected to the Presidency this year whose guiding motto is 'America First.'"[1]
—*William Randolph Hearst, 1932*

into office, Hearst began sending him suggestions about how to run the country. Hearst developed an II-point program that he published daily in his editorial pages. Its basic theme was "Buy American and Spend American."[2] Roosevelt decided he had to be careful with the powerful publisher and gave Hearst access to the White House. The president did not openly discourage Hearst's expectation of being a top-level adviser.

To celebrate Roosevelt's inauguration in January 1933, Hearst used his favorite device for showing his opinions—an editorial-page cartoon. On March 19, the cartoon showed a smiling Uncle Sam leaning over Roosevelt's desk to shake hands with the president as citizens cheered.

Hearst approved of Roosevelt's early legislation to improve the economy, known as the New Deal. However, he feared Congress was giving too much power to the president. Hearst had campaigned for years for government regulation as a way to break up monopolies. But now, he believed that parts of the New Deal would be a disaster because they would impose too many limits on businesses. Hearst was a great believer in free-market capitalism, which had allowed his father and him to make millions.

He thought Roosevelt was endangering the U.S. system of capitalism. He intended to convince the public of that fact.

Winsor McCay, Cartoon Master

The Roosevelt cartoon Hearst published on March 19, 1933, was drawn by Winsor McCay. He was Hearst's favorite illustrator. McCay was a pioneering cartoonist and animator who first drew the famous weekly comic strip *Little Nemo* for the *New York Herald*. In 1911, Hearst hired him to draw for the *New York American*. Impressed by his masterful pen work, Hearst moved McCay to the editorial page, where he was expected to draw cartoons that reinforced Hearst's political views.

McCay's cartoons often stretched across all eight columns of the editorial page. These large drawings held lots of visual interest and complexity. In 1931, McCay's cartoon supporting Hearst's plan to save the economy showed unemployed men afloat on a sea of money, suggesting that the country had money and should spend it on job creation. Another McCay cartoon showed President Herbert Hoover as an old man in a dark suit, his back turned on an endless breadline and throwing a life raft to a sinking Germany.

Newspapers were slow to accept political cartoons, partly because they were difficult to print. With advances in printing technology, crusading editors began to hire their own cartoonists. Hearst was among the first to realize the persuasive power of political cartoons.

By 1933, Hearst's income had dropped from $113 million to $40 million. Most of his newspapers were losing money. Despite this, Hearst refused to sell any of them. Reluctantly, he agreed to his financial adviser's plea to cut spending and wages.

TIES WITH MUSSOLINI AND HITLER

In the early 1930s, Hearst tried

to establish ties with foreign leaders by paying them to write for his "March of Events" Sunday section. One of his writers was Italian dictator Benito Mussolini. Another was German dictator Adolf Hitler. At this time, no one knew that Hitler would start World War II or murder millions of people in the holocaust. Some people considered Hitler a charismatic leader. Many, however, were worried about the violence Hitler's Nazi Party was beginning to cause in Germany.

The Hearst newspapers reported fully on Nazi violence and the worldwide anti-Nazi protest demonstrations. Reporters covered the situation despite German efforts to censor the news. But Hearst cautioned his main German correspondent not to be too critical of Hitler. Still, Hearst opposed Hitler's rise to power. He used Hitler as an example of what might happen if U.S. citizens allowed their democracy to be jeopardized, as Hearst believed was a danger of the New Deal.

In summer 1934, Hearst visited Germany. He met with Hitler in Berlin, rejecting a friend's advice that U.S. citizens would not forgive him for the trip. Apparently, another close friend had encouraged the meeting as a way for Hearst to personally express his

Adolf Hitler, center, and Benito Mussolini, right, marched together in Munich in 1938.

protest of Hitler's anti-Jewish policies. Hearst left Berlin confident that Hitler would mend his ways. He would soon learn that Hitler was not going to follow his advice about the Jews.

Hearst's Crusade against Communism

Hearst's opinions regarding Europe extended beyond Hitler and Germany. Hearst believed European dictators like Hitler were able to rise to power due to a backlash against Communism. Under this political and economic system, government took over private businesses. The United States followed a system of capitalism and deeply opposed the development of Communism.

In March 1934, Hearst had published a series of articles on Communist infiltration in the United States. The articles claimed that Communists had taken over U.S. schools. Hearst called for an investigation. In a signed editorial, Hearst implied a link from labor unions to Communists and from Communists to the Roosevelt administration.

Hearst continued his crusade by threatening to campaign for federal censorship of movies. He worried that movies contained Communist propaganda. He instructed his editors to support all efforts to uncover Communist influence in U.S. life.

Educators, students, and others who disliked Hearst's tactics counterattacked. They led anti-Hearst committees, rallies, and boycotts. Hearst was called a bigot and a Fascist. Fascism is a form of government in which a dictator has total control over the people. His editors feared Hearst was becoming

Hearst on Hitler

Hearst was impressed with Adolf Hitler, as were many people in the 1930s. Hearst wrote, "Hitler certainly is an extraordinary man. We estimate him too lightly in America. He has enormous energy, intense enthusiasm, a marvelous faculty for dramatic oratory, and great organizing ability. Of course all these qualities can be misdirected."[2]

so obsessed with his crusade that his credibility and that of his newspapers was being damaged.

Never deterred by criticism, Hearst continued to publish lists of alleged U.S. Communists. As always, no other opinions were allowed in his newspapers. Hearst declared that he stood for Americanism. Those who disagreed with him should simply not read his papers.

A Candidate to Defeat Roosevelt

Hearst believed getting rid of Roosevelt and his New Deal was essential. Although Hearst approved of putting people back to work doing public projects, he disliked the tremendous costs of Roosevelt's programs. The New Deal was unfair to business, he complained, especially when Roosevelt proposed raising taxes on rich people and corporations.

Hearst also worried that Roosevelt wanted to recognize the World Court. In his daily newspaper criticism, Hearst alternately criticized the president for being a Fascist and a Communist because of the New Deal and his policies toward business. Hearst finally decided that the most effective way to defeat Roosevelt in 1936 would be to find a suitable Republican to run against him. That candidate was

Governor Alf Landon of Kansas. Hearst had never met Landon, but he liked his political record.

Hearst swiftly took direct control of the Landon campaign. His newspapers were blanketed with pictures and admiring articles about Landon. Every day, they ran statistics about Landon's increasing support. Landon easily won the Republican nomination. Hearst then instructed his editors to support the candidate in every way possible. The *New York American*, for example, printed three or four pages daily praising the Republican and attacking Roosevelt and his "Raw Deal."

Hearst on the Economy

Hearst thought economic recovery should come before social justice: "Business people everywhere are sullenly resentful of the needless and useless interference of the administration in the details of business about which they know nothing. . . . Business is also worried about turning the whole country over to the labor unions, and will protest against that at the polls. The labor unions, moreover, are never very grateful."[3]

Despite the Hearst media blitz—or, perhaps, because of it—Franklin Roosevelt won reelection in a landslide. To growing segments of U.S. society, Hearst's support was the kiss of death. By refusing to keep his name and signed editorials out of his papers, Hearst made Roosevelt's many supporters turn away from Hearst's publications in disgust. Hearst attacked labor unions, met with Hitler, and

"I always feel that it is not as important to be consistent as it is to be correct. A man who is completely consistent never learns anything. Conditions change, and he does not."[4]

—*William Randolph Hearst*

spent lavishly during national hard times. Despite his love of the United States and his desire to help people, these actions all damaged Hearst's reputation at least as much as his opposition to World War I.

Working people, once Hearst's most fervent supporters, turned against him. In 1936, Hearst refused to let his editor in Milwaukee, Wisconsin, negotiate a contract with the local chapter of the American Newspaper Guild. This led to a newspaper strike. Then, the guild organized an effective national boycott of Hearst papers. In the past, Hearst had supported newspaper unions, and their members supported him. Now, though, Hearst was convinced that all unions were filled with Communist radicals. The tide had completely turned: Hearst was becoming the symbol of the anti-labor movement.

Franklin Delano Roosevelt, right, rode with Herbert Hoover
to Roosevelt's presidential inauguration in 1933.

The United States entered World War II after Japanese aircraft bombed Pearl Harbor on December 7, 1941.

A Complicated Legacy

ollowing Franklin Roosevelt's huge victory in the 1936 presidential election, William Randolph Hearst was gracious in defeat and tried to make amends. His efforts were too late. The Depression and widespread anger resulting from Hearst's anti-Communist and anti-Roosevelt crusades had led to declining readership. The only part of Hearst's newspaper empire that was still profitable was the Sunday papers, largely because of their comics.

Hearst was in financial trouble because he had not reduced his spending, except for the temporary cuts in spending and wages he had agreed to in 1933. In fact, he had been spending more on real estate and art. Hearst had simply refused to listen to his advisers, trusting that the economy would surely come back stronger. Now, his corporation was drowning in debt.

In 1937, a group of banks moved in to take over the business. Within two years, six daily newspapers had been either sold or closed. Others merged. The International News Service was closed, and film production stopped. A great deal of Hearst's art was sold, which perhaps saddened him most. He lost a large amount of property, too. The construction and most of the parties at San Simeon ceased. According to his son, Hearst made only one public statement about the matter: "I'm a newspaperman. That's all I am, and all I ever want to be. The only thing I really seek now is to be a better newspaperman."[1]

War Objections

In late 1939, Hearst wrote about his strong objections to U.S. involvement in World War II: "I cannot see any legitimate objections to those policies, or any reason for altering them. They are obviously the best policies for the American people, and I am running my papers for the American people. But beyond that they are to my mind the best policies for the welfare of the world."[2]

Hearst's remaining newspapers stayed entirely under his editorial control. In his columns, Hearst argued as he had for years that the United States must stay out of European affairs. In 1939, World War II began in Europe. Hearst's columns urged the United States not to send arms shipments to warring countries. Convinced that Japan was a greater threat than Germany, Hearst urged that the U.S. Pacific coast should be fortified.

Fewer people were listening, however. Hearst's power and influence were reduced. This was partly because of his widely publicized financial troubles. It was also because he had alienated himself from both political parties and his working-class supporters.

Hearst's concerns about Japan were realized in 1941. On December 7, the Japanese bombed Pearl Harbor in Hawaii. The next day, Hearst abruptly ended his isolationist fight and urged an all-out effort to win the war. Ironically, the United States' entry into World War II saved Hearst's newspapers, although he had done everything possible to prevent

U.S. involvement. The growing wartime economy brought increased advertising and circulation. Hearst found a new source of profit by licensing his comic characters—especially Popeye and Blondie—for radio, animation, children's books, and novelty items. He was able to buy back much of his corporation's stock and pay off his major creditors.

OLD AGE

Hearst's financial crisis ended by 1945. Although his empire was a lot smaller, he still had many assets. Hearst had 17 daily newspapers—with a

Citizen Kane

The modern image of Hearst was strongly affected by an unflattering depiction of the publisher in the 1941 film *Citizen Kane*. The movie was the project of a man nearly as famous as Hearst: Orson Welles. Welles told a story about a Hearst-like newspaper publisher. Hearst was then very unpopular due to his attacks on Franklin Roosevelt and his Communist witch hunts.

Citizen Kane tells the story of a ruthless, powerful newspaper publisher who ends up bitter and alone in his gloomy castle. When Hearst's Hollywood gossip columnist, Louella Parsons, saw a print of the film, she was outraged. With Hearst's go-ahead, but without his direct participation, Louella Parsons spearheaded a mostly private campaign to prevent the opening of *Citizen Kane*. Rumors flew that the Hearst press would expose Communists in Hollywood. A mid-February premiere in New York was cancelled. Finally, on May 1, 1941, the film was released, although major distributors were afraid to show it. After all that, *Citizen Kane* was a critical but not a popular success. Although it now appears on many lists of the greatest movies ever made, the film's camera and storytelling techniques were too far ahead of its time to be appreciated when it was released.

Thousands of mourners attended Hearst's funeral in San Francisco.

combined circulation of 5 million—12 magazines, 4 radio stations, a wire service, a feature service, and a Sunday supplement.

Reinvigorated at the age of 82, he returned to his home at San Simeon and started building again. Family and friends visited often, and Hearst remained involved in every detail of his life and surroundings. He enjoyed his grandchildren. He wrote a will in 1947 but was not ready for retirement.

He stopped writing signed columns. However, he still approved major editorials and sent editorial outlines to his writers.

When Hearst developed heart trouble, he was advised by his doctors to move closer to Los Angeles hospitals. In 1947, he left San Simeon forever to live in Beverly Hills, a neighborhood of Los Angeles.

Hearst was growing too frail to supervise his newspapers closely. His New York editors, including his son William Jr., pushed the anti-Communist crusade further than Hearst would have permitted. Hearst kept working, sending suggestions by telegraph to his son and other staff members, but he had largely lost editorial control to his son and others of like mind.

At the age of 88, Hearst died on August 14, 1951. Nearly 1,500 people attended his funeral at Grace Episcopal Cathedral in San Francisco. Many more crowded outside the church. He was buried near his parents at a cemetery outside San Francisco, the city of his birth and his first newspaper.

The Great Innovator

At the time of his death, the strongest parts of Hearst's empire were the ones least identified with the publisher—his magazines, the Sunday supplement, and the syndicated feature service. Most of his newspapers were sold or shut down after his death. In 2009, though, Hearst Corporation owned 16 daily newspapers, 15 magazines, numerous television and radio stations, and various Internet businesses.

Without a doubt, Hearst was the leading journalist of his day. He organized the nation's largest chain of newspapers and formed international news, photo, and feature services to support each of them. These services also sold material to other newspapers and magazines. He increased readership by producing the most entertaining newspapers around. Hearst hired the finest editors, reporters, writers, illustrators, and political cartoonists in the country and gave them public credit and job security. He also hired many female journalists.

Life of a Journalist

Hearst summed up his early days as a newspaperman: "Those were the wonderful days and happy achievements of youth. No grandiose performance of later years ever equaled them in satisfaction. Life . . . was one wonderful adventure after another. The competition of journalism was a glad sport; and yet back of it all was a due sense of responsibility—a genuine desire to use the powers and opportunities of the press to serve and to save."[3]

Hearst worked ceaselessly to improve his product with the latest printing technology. He perfected the use of large, attention-grabbing headlines. His use of larger type and fewer columns made newspapers easier to read. He was an influential pioneer in quality illustrations.

Hearst's newspapers identified with their communities, promoting improvements and highlighting local success stories. He offered something for everyone: sports, fashion, advice columns, weather forecasts, high society, games, contests, and serialized literature. He loved and championed comic strips, presenting them in color and encouraging innovative approaches. Today's newspapers reflect Hearst's innovations in many ways.

Hearst believed in government by newspaper, and he wanted to be president. He played by his own rules and, at the height of his

"He considered himself a self-made man, because, like his father and his mother, he invented himself: as art collector, builder, journalist, publisher, and politician. His ambitions were limitless, but so too were his talents and resources. He was in all things defined by contradiction, larger than life."[4]

—David Nasaw,
Hearst biographer

career, forced others to play by them also. Hearst's newspapers reflected his ideas and trumpeted his name. He was not interested in objectivity. Hearst believed he spoke for the U.S. public, even when his own opinions became increasingly different from those of his readers. He used the power of the press to influence both the lives of everyday readers and the policies of government at every level.

Hearst was a talented, ambitious man who passionately pursued his personal and professional interests. He used his fortune to do what he felt was best for himself, his readers, and his country—regardless of whether others agreed with him. And though he had friends and enemies alike throughout his many years, William Randolph Hearst's place in U.S. history is undeniable.

William Randolph Hearst left a lasting legacy in publishing and in U.S. history.

Timeline

1863	1883	1887
William Randolph Hearst is born in San Francisco on April 29.	Hearst becomes business manager of the *Harvard Lampoon.*	Hearst takes over the *San Francisco Examiner* in March.

1900	1901	1902
Hearst publishes the first issue of the *Chicago American* on July 4. He campaigns for Bryan and attacks McKinley.	Hearst is blamed for the McKinley assassination. He changes the name of the *Journal* to the *American.*	Hearst is elected to the U.S. House of Representatives.

1895

Hearst buys the *New York Morning Journal.* His first issue is November 7.

1896

Hearst hires Pulitzer's entire Sunday staff, including the Yellow Kid cartoonist. He supports Bryan for president.

1898

Hearst and Pulitzer engage in a circulation war by publicizing Spain's brutal treatment of Cubans.

1903

Hearst marries Millicent Willson on April 28. They will have five sons.

1904

Hearst does not receive the Democratic nomination for president, but he is reelected to Congress.

1905

Hearst forms a political party, the Municipal Ownership League. He loses the race for mayor of New York City.

TIMELINE

1906	1909	1914
Hearst runs for governor of New York and loses.	Hearst loses his bid for New York mayor. Hearst creates the International News Service to coordinate his syndication services.	Hearst begins his campaign to keep the United States out of World War I.

1921	1930	1934
Hearst begins a newspaper-buying spree, adding 16 papers by 1925.	Hearst moves his business headquarters to San Simeon. He begins a campaign to keep the United States out of European affairs.	In the summer, Hearst meets with Hitler. Hearst begins his anti-Communist crusade.

1915	1919	1920
Hearst forms a features service, King Feature Service. He meets Marion Davies, who becomes his companion.	Hearst's mother dies, leaving him a fortune. He builds Cosmopolitan Studio in New York and begins work on San Simeon.	Hearst opposes the League of Nations and endorses his first Republican presidential candidate, Warren G. Harding.

1937	1945	1951
Hearst gives up control of his business to avoid bankruptcy. Many of his assets are sold, including art and property.	Hearst's financial crisis ends. He returns to San Simeon and begins building again.	Hearst dies in Beverly Hills, California, on August 14.

ESSENTIAL FACTS

DATE OF BIRTH

April 29, 1863

PLACE OF BIRTH

San Francisco, California

DATE OF DEATH

August 14, 1951

PARENTS

George Hearst and Phoebe Apperson Hearst

EDUCATION

Private tutors, St. Paul's Episcopal School, Harvard University

MARRIAGE

Millicent Willson (1903)

CHILDREN

George, William Randolph Jr., John, Randolph, David

Career Highlights

Hearst created a media empire that included newspapers, magazines, a film studio, a syndication service, and radio and television stations. As a publisher, he changed the look of newspapers with the use of large, bold headlines and illustrations. Newspapers today still use this style. In addition, Hearst offered his staff multiyear contracts and encouraged bylines. He was the first newspaper publisher to do so.

Societal Contribution

As a publisher and a politician, Hearst used his newspapers to advocate causes to help average citizens. He also advocated women's suffrage and an eight-hour workday through his newspapers. His appeal to immigrants, support for labor unions, and demand for reforms made him a powerful political force.

Conflicts

Although initially a Democrat, Hearst's frustration and disgust with both major political parties prompted him to form his own party. He returned to the Democrats when his party failed to gain influence. Later, he supported Republican candidates for president before returning to the Democratic Party a final time. Some of the publisher's actions and opinions caused a drop in readership, including his stance against both world wars and his crusade against Communism.

Quote

"I'm a newspaperman. That's all I am, and all I ever want to be. The only thing I really seek now is to be a better newspaperman."
—*William Randolph Hearst*

ADDITIONAL RESOURCES

SELECT BIBLIOGRAPHY

Hearst, William Randolph. *William Randolph Hearst: A Portrait in His Own Words.* Ed. Edmond Coblentz. New York: Simon and Schuster, 1952.

Hearst, William Randolph, Jr., and Jack Casserly. *The Hearsts: Father and Son.* Niwot, CO: Roberts Rinehart, 1991.

Nasaw, David. *The Chief: The Life of William Randolph Hearst.* Boston: Houghton Mifflin, 2000.

Procter, Ben. *William Randolph Hearst: The Early Years, 1863–1910.* New York: Oxford UP, 1998.

Procter, Ben. *William Randolph Hearst: The Later Years, 1911–1951.* New York: Oxford UP, 2007.

Swanberg, W. A. *Citizen Hearst: A Biography of William Randolph Hearst.* New York: Charles Scribner's Sons, 1961.

FURTHER READING

Cohen, Daniel. *Yellow Journalism: Scandal, Sensationalism and Gossip in the Media.* Minneapolis: Twenty-First Century, 2000.

Hamil, Pete. *News Is a Verb: Journalism at the End of the 20th Century.* New York: Ballantine, 1998.

Whitelaw, Nancy. *William Randolph Hearst and the American Century.* Greensboro: Morgan Reynolds, 2004.

Web Sites

To learn more about William Randolph Hearst, visit ABDO Publishing Company online at **www.abdopublishing.com**. Web sites about William Randolph Hearst are featured on our Book Links page. These links are routinely monitored and updated to provide the most current information available.

Places to Visit

Hearst Castle
750 Hearst Castle Road, San Simeon, CA 93452-9740
805-927-2020
www.hearstcastle.org
William Randolph Hearst's stately manor is open to the public and includes tours and exhibits on the journalist's life.

Hearst Tower
300 West 57th Street, New York, NY 10019
www.hearst.com
Built on top of the original 1928 Hearst building, the 2006 tower is the current home of Hearst Publications.

Newseum
555 Pennsylvania Avenue NW, Washington, DC 20001
888-639-7386
www.newseum.org
The museum presents five centuries of news history with hands-on exhibits.

Glossary

activist
Someone in favor of direct, vigorous action regarding an issue or program.

boycott
An organized refusal to buy or support something.

capitalism
An economic system in which individuals own businesses and property.

circulation
The number of readers; readership.

Communism
An economic system in which there is no private property and the state owns businesses, farms, and factories.

crusade
An enthusiastic campaign to improve or remedy something.

Fascism
A system of government that prizes race and nation and is led by a dictator who has complete control over the people.

isolationist
A person who believes the country should stay out of international alliances.

League of Nations
An international organization established by the peace treaties that ended World War I; its purpose was the promotion of world peace and security.

masthead
The information in a newspaper that gives the title and details of ownership, advertising rates, and subscription rates.

municipal
Relating to local or city government.

New Deal
> The legislative program of President Franklin Roosevelt designed to promote economic recovery and social reform during the 1930s.

progressive
> In favor of social improvement by government action.

reform
> An improvement in what is defective or corrupt; ending a social problem by introducing a better course of action.

syndication
> Selling materials for publication in a number of newspapers at the same time; a group of newspapers under one management.

Tammany Hall
> The Democratic Party political machine that controlled New York City politics until the mid-1930s.

witch hunt
> The searching for and harassing of political opponents or people one does not agree with.

yellow journalism
> A negative term to describe the use of unethical practices or exaggerated, inaccurate reporting to sell newspapers.

Source Notes

Chapter 1. A Stolen Election
1. David Nasaw. *The Chief: The Life of William Randolph Hearst.* Boston: Houghton Mifflin, 2000. 197.
2. Ben Procter. *William Randolph Hearst: The Early Years, 1863–1910.* New York: Oxford UP, 1998. x.
3. David Nasaw. *The Chief: The Life of William Randolph Hearst.* Boston: Houghton Mifflin, 2000. 200.

Chapter 2. Boomtown Boy
1. W. A. Swanberg. *Citizen Hearst: A Biography of William Randolph Hearst.* New York: Charles Scribner's Sons, 1961. 40.
2. William Randolph Hearst Jr., and Jack Casserly. *The Hearsts: Father and Son.* Niwot, CO: Robert's Rinehart Publishers, 1991. 15.
3. Ibid. 11.

Chapter 3. Monarch of the Dailies
1. William Randolph Hearst. *William Randolph Hearst: A Portrait in His Own Words.* Ed. Edmond D. Coblentz. New York: Simon and Schuster, 1952. 28.
2. Ben Procter. *William Randolph Hearst: The Early Years, 1863–1910.* New York: Oxford UP, 1998. 46.
3. David Nasaw. *The Chief: The Life of William Randolph Hearst.* Boston: Houghton Mifflin, 2000. 75.
4. William Randolph Hearst Jr., and Jack Casserly. *The Hearsts: Father and Son.* Niwot, CO: Robert's Rinehart, 1991. 14.

Chapter 4. Newspaper Wars
1. Ben Procter. *William Randolph Hearst: The Early Years, 1863-1910.* New York: Oxford UP, 1998. 82.
2. David Nasaw. *The Chief: The Life of William Randolph Hearst.* Boston: Houghton Mifflin, 2000. 127.

Chapter 5. Running for Office

1. David Nasaw. *The Chief: The Life of William Randolph Hearst.* Boston: Houghton Mifflin, 2000. 174.
2. Ibid. 211.

Chapter 6. Questions of Loyalty

1. William Randolph Hearst. *William Randolph Hearst: A Portrait in His Own Words.* Ed. by Edmond D. Coblentz. New York: Simon and Schuster, 1952. 254.
2. David Nasaw. *The Chief: The Life of William Randolph Hearst.* Boston: Houghton Mifflin, 2000. 242.
3. Ben Procter. *William Randolph Hearst: The Later Years, 1911–1951.* New York: Oxford UP, 2007. 46.
4. W.A. Swanberg. *Citizen Hearst: A Biography of William Randolph Hearst.* New York: Charles Scribner's Sons, 1961. 349.
5. William Randolph Hearst. *William Randolph Hearst: A Portrait in His Own Words.* Ed. by Edmond D. Coblentz. New York: Simon and Schuster, 1952. 84.

Chapter 7. New and Old Alliances

1. David Nasaw. *The Chief: The Life of William Randolph Hearst.* Boston: Houghton Mifflin, 2000. 273.
2. Ibid. 283.
3. David Nasaw. *The Chief: The Life of William Randolph Hearst.* Boston: Houghton Mifflin, 2000. 391.
4. Ben Procter. *William Randolph Hearst: The Later Years, 1911–1951.* New York: Oxford UP, 2007. 98.

Source Notes Continued

Chapter 8. Trials of the Thirties
1. William Randolph Hearst. *William Randolph Hearst: A Portrait in His Own Words.* Ed. Edmond D. Coblentz. New York: Simon and Schuster, 1952. 40.
2. Ibid. 106.
3. Ibid. 162.
4. David Nasaw. *The Chief: The Life of William Randolph Hearst.* Boston: Houghton Mifflin, 2000. ix.

Chapter 9. A Complicated Legacy
1. William Randolph Hearst Jr., and Jack Casserly. *The Hearsts: Father and Son.* Niwot, CO: Robert's Rinehart, 1991. 59.
2. William Randolph Hearst. *William Randolph Hearst: A Portrait in His Own Words.* Ed. Edmond D. Coblentz. New York: Simon and Schuster, 1952. 209.
3. Ibid. 48.
4. David Nasaw. *The Chief: The Life of William Randolph Hearst.* Boston: Houghton Mifflin, 2000. xiii.

INDEX

Index Continued

About the Author

Bonnie Z. Goldsmith has long been writing and editing materials for students and teachers. She took time out to teach English as a second language for six years. She lives in Minneapolis, Minnesota, and loves cats, reading, writing poetry, and traveling.

Photo Credits

AP Images, cover, 40, 43, 73, 95; Library of Congress, 6, 10, 23, 31, 44, 48, 53, 63, 64, 85; Corbis, 15; Frances Benjamin Johnston/Library of Congress, 16; Time & Life Pictures/Getty Images, 24, 68; North Wind Picture Archives, 27, 54; Hulton Archive/Getty Images, 32; Swim Ink 2, LLC/Corbis, 36; Bettmann/Corbis, 60, 74, 90; Dea Picture Library/Photo Library, 80; 3LH-B&W/Photo Library, 86